MW00936786

ACHY-BREAKY BACK

A QUICK GUIDE FOR ALL STAGES OF BACK PAIN

ARNIE HOLTZ

BALBOA.PRESS

A DIVISION OF HAY HOUSE

Balboa Press books may be ordered through booksellers or by contacting:

Balboa Press
A Division of Hay House
1663 Liberty Drive
Bloomington, IN 47403
www.balboapress.com
844-682-1282

Because of the dynamic nature of the Internet, any web addresses or links contained in this book may have changed since publication and may no longer be valid. The views expressed in this work are solely those of the author and do not necessarily reflect the views of the publisher, and the publisher hereby disclaims any responsibility for them.

The author of this book does not dispense medical advice or prescribe the use of any technique as a form of treatment for physical, emotional, or medical problems without the advice of a physician, either directly or indirectly. The intent of the author is only to offer information of a general nature to help you in your quest for emotional and spiritual well-being. In the event you use any of the information in this book for yourself, which is your constitutional right, the author and the publisher assume no responsibility for your actions.

Any people depicted in stock imagery provided by Getty Images are models, and such images are being used for illustrative purposes only. Certain stock imagery © Getty Images.

Print information available on the last page.

ISBN: 978-1-9822-7294-4 (sc)
ISBN: 978-1-9822-7296-8 (hc)
ISBN: 978-1-9822-7295-1 (e)

Library of Congress Control Number: 2021916311

Balboa Press rev. date: 09/17/2021

Everything should be made as simple
as possible, but not simpler.

—Albert Einstein

CONTENTS

PREFACE

I began writing this book a few years ago, not knowing that by the time of its completion, the world would be in the middle of a coronavirus pandemic affecting every aspect of life for billions of people. It is now October 2020, and this book is going to initial editing. The timing is perfect as many of us are going through unprecedented uncertainty and stress with many people in financial crisis and insecurity. I am not aware of statistics showing us how many people are experiencing back pain due to the coronavirus's insecurities and stresses. However, I feel that many people globally are suffering, and this book will be vital to them. I base this presumption that stress, uncertainty, and financial woes will create an emotional response that will manifest into physical ailments, such as back weakness and dysfunction.

ACKNOWLEDGMENTS

I acknowledge with deep gratitude all of my great teachers, patients, family members, and friends who contributed to this book's writing. Without them, the task would have been impossible to accomplish.

Thanks to Jean Loving, my first influential massage therapy teacher, who opened my mind to touch and its effects on the connective tissue system. Another influential teacher, Dr. Michael Shea, introduced me to delicate, sensitive, healing, energetic touch. I would never have become an accomplished bodyworker without the guidance and instructions from my following teachers: George Kousaleos, LMT, owner of the Core Institute, Tallahassee, Florida; William Bonney, PhD; Gary Genna, LMT; Thomas W. Wing, DC, ND, LAc; Dennis Greenlee, DC, LAc; Eric Dalton, PhD, LMT; James Waslaski, LMT; Thomas Myers, LMT; Jim Asher, LMT; Aaron Mattis, MS, RKT, LMT; and Kenzo Kase, DC.

I would also like to thank the many published authors, innovators, and researchers who have significantly influenced my career. I give thanks to Leon Chaitow, ND, DO; Dr. Tiffany Fields, who taught me the essence of human touch; Dr. Milton Trager; Deane Juhan, LMT, author of *Job's Body;* and Dr. Ida Rolf, founder of the Rolf Institute and creator of myofascial structural integration. Thank you to Dr. Florence Licatta for not only being a friend and terrific chiropractor but for expertise on human physiology and back pain, upon which I leaned significantly. Thanks to my dear friends and fellow massage therapists Paul Pock and JoAnn Fekany, for the many hours spent on their tables getting bodywork and many hours spent in conversation on myofascial bodywork.

I would also like to mention my dearly departed aunt Viola, who unknowingly became the primary influencer in my career change to massage therapy. She told me that I had magical hands when I was a very young boy; I used to massage her and many of my first cousins. Her words played a significant role in thinking of what I wanted to be next in my life at age forty-nine. "It's never too late," as they say. This book is only possible because of the road I decided to take at age forty-nine. I love you, Josh and Jordan, my two sons who supported me during my career change.

My first inspiration to become a healer came from my father, Dr. Harry Holtz, an eye surgeon who taught me while growing up compassion and empathy toward people in need. No physician had a better bedside manner and an enormous following of adoring patients than my father, a man with a compassionate heart. My thanks to my mother, who taught me to follow my dreams and to never quit.

Lastly, my deepest thanks and love to my precious wife, Dr. Mary Holtz, who has been with me on my journey since 1993 and without whose support and love I never would be at this beautiful point in my life. I will always cherish the years spent together in our practice, day after day, healing those in need. She is my healer and muse.

INTRODUCTION

This book aims to prevent the reader from making the same mistakes I made during my lifetime of back pain. This book is a quick, easy-to-read, easy-to-understand, and comprehensive guide to the proper care of your back when experiencing painful episodes and to prevent them from repeating. This book was written in an informal style precisely like I would address my clients, purposely leaving out complex physiological terminology and concepts.

The reader will understand the anatomical, physiological, and emotional aspects of back pain. More so, the reader will understand the importance of the body-mind connection to back pain. This book's information results from my lifelong back pain experiences and cumulative knowledge and skills as a licensed massage therapist specializing in successfully treating pain, myoskeletal misalignments, and limited movement patterns.

The opening section will detail my personal history of back pain, including the physical traumas and the emotions that perpetuated this condition. An in-depth discourse follows as to the how and why of back pain. Next, there will be a step-by-step guide on what to do and what not to do while in the different back pain stages. This book will explain how to choose effective medical interventions during and after back pain episodes to lessen the risk of future episodes.

My earnest hope—as it is my belief—is that this book will serve as a shining example and striking healing lesson to all readers, allowing them to realize the natural self-healing ability inside them. With this hope and blessing, I send it out into the universe with love and admiration for all who find it and are helped by it.

MY STORY

The nature of back pain is bewildering even to medical professionals. Back pain is not always objective; it can be subjective in many ways. Pain is subjective and has many gray areas, such as each phase's length, how intensely it's felt, and its recognition. Back pain can be either a new experience occurring once in a lifetime or a reoccurring experience. Back pain can be an extremely debilitating experience or just a low-level ache with accompanying stiffness.

Back pain can locate in the mid and lower back. One section can affect the other. The back pain discussed in this book is that of the lower back, the lumbar region just above the pelvic bone. The lumbar spine has five joints connected to a sixth joint called the sacrum. This book will cover all aspects of lower back pain, from the worst to mild and from the singular event to repetitive occurrences.

An understanding of your low back pain needs to begin with my story. You'll see that the origin of back pain can come from an earlier incident many years before its current presentation. The experience can be purely physical or emotional, or as often happens, they are both connected as one. For me, it was both a traumatic physical and emotional experience.

My story began as an eleven-year-old camper at an overnight camp. I experienced a violent beating by my much older counselor for a mistaken irresponsible behavior. He bent me over a bed and twice struck me very hard with the wooden end of a broomstick on my bare lower back and buttocks. I will always remember my fear of being helpless as I saw him reach for the broomstick.

Sixty-five years later, I still remember the pain of the beating, the helplessness, and the fear, but I now recognize the emotional attachments and how they carried through my whole life, affecting my health and the decisions I made. I recall the fear, shame, humiliation, hate for him, and hate for myself for not standing up. Being young and healthy, I eventually recovered from the physical pain, or so I thought. The emotional pain, however, ultimately manifested itself into my first severe back episode ten years later. In the decades to follow, I suffered terribly with repeated back pain. Let me show you how it played out.

I was twenty-one and almost out of college. I was a mental and physical wreck. Physically I was overweight and out of shape. Mentally, I was anxious and stressed because I had no idea what I wanted to do with the rest of my life, and here I was about to graduate college in a major I had no attachment to. I also felt pressure from a relationship I was slowly committing to even though it didn't feel right. These stressful circumstances all pointed to one thing: my lack of emotional self-support.

My first full-blown, severe, back episode was inevitable. That episode occurred while working a summer job that required loading heavy liquor cartons manually onto trucks. I began to notice a tightening in my lower back two weeks before my experience, but I needed the money to buy my first car so I persevered. My first back episode's physical impetus was the hard labor, and the emotional impetus was the lingering issue of nonsupport.

My mind subconsciously remembered that young camper's physical and emotional pain manifested into my body as an internal environment of tight, unyielding muscles and fascia. Brain memories manifesting into physical trauma are called the body-mind sequence and referred to as psychosomatic. This sequence is mentioned over and over again throughout this book.

It was a no-brainer that sooner rather than later my back would go out. It only took lifting that one extra carton for it to happen. For the next twenty-six years, I continued to do everything wrong for a chronically injured back. I mean *everything*. Nothing in my life was in balance with my true self, except for my two sons' love. Wrongful medical care also contributed to my woes.

The two doctors I initially went to for treatment misdiagnosed my condition. Neither doctor took an x-ray, and each diagnosed my condition on presentation alone. One doctor prescribed two days of rest and heat over my lower back, and the other doctor's advice was to be on the "bottom" when having sex, not on top. They both diagnosed me as having a strained lower back. The correct diagnosis should have been left-sided posterolateral disc herniation of L4-5 and L5-6 with right sciatic nerve impingement.

I rested for two days with heat and continued working for three more weeks as a janitor cleaning broken glass and liquids off the assembly line floor. The result was I suffered on and off (more on than off) repeatedly with severe back pain for the next ten years. These horrific episodes would put me flat on my back in bed for days at a time, unable to move. The pain alone created even more stress and tension. For nine of those ten years, I was involved either in heavy labor or standing on my feet from early morning to after dinnertime six to seven days a week.

It was not until I received competent medical care at the world-renowned Kessler Institute in New Jersey that I finally began the healing road to correcting my back. To this day, I am grateful to the great, effective care of Dr. Sullivan and his physical therapists. I was finally diagnosed correctly and treated accordantly. For the next twenty years, my episodes continued but with less frequency and with less downtime. I had finally turned the corner. Little did I know that one day I would be a healer helping others with their back pain.

After thirty years of experiencing back pain and twenty-eight years of successfully performing hands-on psychosomatic, orthopedic massage/bodywork to thousands of clients, I feel compelled to write this book and share my gained knowledge of back pain management. I hope that this book helps back pain sufferers avoid the mistakes I made and make life's transitions easier.

CHAPTER 1
THE WHY OF BACK PAIN

Eighty percent of the world's population will experience an episode of low back pain at least once in their lives. Why? Why is back pain so globally prevalent? What could be so universal as to affect 80 percent of the world's population? What would the vast majority of people experience as a whole? It is common to hear people say, "I have a bad back" or "My back went out." Physiologically, neither thought is correct. Your back is good, and it is doing its job, which is preventing you from further damaging it. No, your back didn't go out. Where would it go anyway? "Went out" means the now weakened lower back is so tight and bound it can no longer appropriately function, essentially painfully putting you out of commission.

Why we experience a "bad back" that "goes out" requires us to know the many contributing factors. Let's look at our low back stresses. Let's think of back pain as a soup that we are

1

making. Let's start with the two most essential ingredients: an endless, lifetime supply of gravity and atmospheric weight, both pushing down on our bodies. Another ingredient is the natural aging process to be discussed further. Next, is a lifetime worth of physical traumas and emotional stresses. Humans experience accidents, falls, fights, deep wounds, physical/emotional abuse, work/home-related stress, money worries, overcrowding, global pandemics, political/social friction, and the general chaos of life. To blend all of the ingredients, we add the stock, the central nervous system. Now it's clear so many people experience back pain at least once in their lifetime.

So lesson one is to be always aware, pay attention, and listen to your body. Stress traumas, whether emotional or physical, will set up a responding neural pattern in the body's tissues, specifically muscle, tendon, ligament, and bone. Once traumatized, muscle tissue will retain this neural memory to protect the spine and nerve roots. This process is called tissue memory. Muscle memory appears to make the muscles feel stronger, but they are not. Yes, they are very tight and unyielding, but this is not strength. Physiologically, for a muscle to be powerful, it first needs to be flexible, enabling the fibers within to expand and contract fully.

Back issues for most people begin in their midtwenties. It is about this age in our physical development that our bones and muscles become fully developed. The natural flexibility that we once had as younger people is first beginning to lessen. The effects of our natural aging process begin to make their presence felt. The aging process starts with the drying and tightening of our bodily tissues, most notably the muscles, tendons, and ligaments. We begin to feel the heavy demands of gravity on our bodies, thus creating skeletal structural misalignments. Our past childhood stress traumas contribute to this overall tightening process, such as the stresses of modern-day life, work, family, and relationships. All of the above factors are called psychosomatic influencers.

We all have an inner voice called intuition. When we pay close attention to ourselves and listen to this inner voice, we can head off the most debilitating back pain episodes. I believe that all back pain is linked to some stressful emotions, even when a physical trauma is involved. I am not alone in this thinking. In history, the philosopher Plato taught his students about the mind-body concept. Today, psychoneuroimmunology is a field of medicine that links the body's ills to the mind and spirit. More and more, allopathic medicine is taking notice of the whole body's health and the alternatives to pharmaceutical drugs. An entire branch of medicine has arisen in the past few decades that adheres to this approach, and it is called functional medicine.

The most important concept to remember in body-mind therapy is that the mind and the body are one. What goes through the mind will go through the body, and what affects the body will affect the mind. What affects the body-mind the most is stress. Living in constant tension as most of us do will lead to chronically tight body tissues and painful back episodes.

The psychosomatic (mind-body) influences that initiated my back pain episode are common to all of us. Forces that threaten us will activate a fight-or-flight response in our sympathetic nervous system. Fear is the most common influencer. The sympathetic nerves will prepare us for fight or flight by increasing adrenaline production and sending more blood to our periphery muscles (legs and arms). The fight-or-flight response system is nature's way of preserving life. This lifesaving response no longer pertains to facing sabertooth tigers in our modern age, but it does pertain to stressful emotions. Let us face it: we do have an overabundance of stress in our everyday lives—tons of pressure.

Unresolved negative emotions and unrelenting stress are the crux of our problem. Carrying these unresolved negative emotions through life, in turn, perpetuates the mind-body fight-or-flight response that will chronically and permanently tighten muscles, tendons, and ligaments. There are many destructive effects of stress on our bodies, but we will only discuss the musculoskeletal system for this book's purpose.

Stress and negativity are so prevalent in our modern, fast-paced world that most of us are in a constant state of fight or flight. Technology companies try to make life easier and quicker for us, but is this pace healthy? We also have constant pressure from monetary issues to political differences, environmental influences, and so on. The effect of this continuous sympathetic nervous activation is an exhausted and weakened body that includes all of its systems and organs, not the least of which is the neuromuscular system.

As said, continuous fight-or-flight sympathetic responses will stress our entire body and tighten shortened muscles will then pull on the bones to which they are attached. Added to the constant fight-or-flight syndrome is the body's struggle with gravitational weight and the body's response to physical traumas. These conditions will create the perfect achy-breaky back event, but this book's focus is mostly on nonsupport of self. A person who denies their truth is lost in life and will make poor decisions, all of which creates a continuous, negative emotional mind-body stress. That was my life for fifty-five years. Hopefully, it will not be yours.

Unresolved emotional stresses relating to nonsupport, whether from ourselves or outside circumstances, will always manifest in lower back weakness and pain. Tissue memories were instantly activated, responding to issues of nonsupport. Anyone going through a lengthy period of insecurity and uncertainty will almost always have a back that "goes out."

Physical stress traumas also play an essential role in low back pain. Physical stress traumas are not always the obvious ones, such as accidents and lifting heavyweights. Physical stress traumas, specifically to the lower back, can be attributed to biomechanical dysfunctions, muscle overload, and poor posture. All three stresses in some parts are related.

Biomechanical dysfunction simply means the inarticulation of joints in demand movement. Are there inarticulations of the spinal joints due to the uneven push and pulls of the attached muscles, and will the articulations cause pain and inflammation? Coupled to biomechanical dysfunction are overloading of the back muscles and poor posture.

Overloading the back muscles means they are in a constant state of demand-response contraction. This overloading will cause tight, exhausted muscles to weaken. The low back muscles have the responsibility of supporting the upright posture and the action of the legs. Body posture displaying a forward head, forward chest, forward shoulders, and rounded back will always produce excess strain on the low back. Stressing the lower back muscles can also be attributed to the arm and shoulder movements that require these muscles' support. Influencing forces exerted by the shoulders and arms that need support from the back muscles will also stress those muscles. Understanding why we experience low back pain leads us to understand how it occurs in the body.

CHAPTER 2
THE HOW OF BACK PAIN

Our body tissues have an essential role in the how of back pain. What would be your guess as to the involved tissue of back pain? Would the tissue be muscle, tendon, ligament, bone, or nerve? If you guessed all five, you would be right. A healthy back must demonstrate four necessary tissue conditions: muscle flexibility, right muscle tone, unimpeded blood flow, and unimpeded nerve conduction. Correct and effective care of our body is essential for good back health.

The how of back pain begins as a progression of neuromuscular responses to stress. First, stressed muscle tissue responding to brain messages will tighten and shorten. The tightened muscles will then pull on the bones they're attached to, which then press on the nerves nearest to them, causing inflammation and pain. Back pain emanates not only from inflammation but also from the tight muscles themselves. It's like a cycle of never-ending pain: muscle tightness then inflammation back to tightness. The affected tissues in low back pain are the muscles, tendons, ligaments, bones, and nerves from the spine, ribs, and pelvis. You would be surprised to know that all of these tissues are of one family called connective tissue.

Connective tissue is so prevalent in the human anatomy that we wouldn't have a shape, stability, movement, or life without it. The very first development in the fetus in gestation is the organization of connective tissue. Connective tissue is all-encompassing. It is a continuous web of fabric that has no beginning or end. Connective tissue has many subtypes that can be as hard as bone and as liquid as blood plasma. Connective tissue binds and holds the body in place, connects all moving parts enabling movement, and connects bone to bone, muscle to bone, and nerves to bone/muscle. Let me draw you a picture of what the continuous web of connective looks like in the body.

Imagine a void. Imagine one by one the skeletal bones float in from skull to foot, but they are not connected yet. They are just floating there in space in their proper anatomical order. Next, let's imagine the organs float in and take their accurate anatomical space, again not attached but just floating along with the bones. Now the muscles flow into their proper anatomical placements, and at the ends of these muscles are tendons. These tendons then magically attach the muscles to the bones, and appearing next are the ligaments that connect the bones to the bones. Is the body complete? What is missing? Nerves, blood vessels, and lymph vessels? Let's put them all in.

So now we see floating bones connected to floating muscles connected to another by ligaments. We see floating organs, blood vessels, and lymph vessels. How will all of these correctly positioned floating parts come together as one? The answer is a connective tissue in the form of a white, watery, very flexible tissue that finds its place in the body. Now all of the muscles, organs, bones, vessels, and nerves are continuously connected, united, and fluid in motion.

Suddenly, a whole human body is formed, but another layer of connective tissue is needed to connect the skin to the inside body. Imagine under the skin is a liquid mesh bodystocking with no beginning and end. Lastly, the skin and hair float in to cover the whole body. This complete image is the entire human body. Connective tissue is so prevalent that if we remove it from our imagined body, all that will be left is a pile of skin and hair lying in a heap on the floor.

Connective tissue has many different subtypes, each having its composition and function. The subtype called fascia is the focus of this book. What does fascia look like? It comprises three main components: water, collagen, and a wet, cellular ground substance called matrix. These three components are the structural foundation of all connective tissue. One can see collagen as a tile on a wall and the ground substance, matrix, is the grout that holds them in place. The ratio of collagen to water to the matrix will determine the structure of fascia. More collagen and less water and matrix will make fascia dense, thick, and strong, and the opposite applies; the more water and matrix, the more liquid and flexible the fascia. In its most fluid form, fascia lets the muscles slide against one another as it connects muscle to muscle. Fascia, in its most liquid state, can be found in the bone marrow as plasma. Fascia, in its dense form, is bone and ligament.

Fascia is present in the muscle, bone, ligament, and nerves wrapping around the outside and inside of a muscle, determining its flexibility, contraction speed, and release speed. It then connects the muscle to the bone and wraps around the bone. The bone and the marrow within are also fasciae. Nerves are wrapped in fascia and then connected to the muscle and bone by fascia. Put merely, the connective tissue is like the parent and bone and muscle and nerve are the children. Fascia is part of the central nervous system communicating messages from the muscles and bones to the brain.

Fascia communicates with the brain through activating specialized cells called fibroblasts. These cells can then change the composition of the surrounding fascia based upon stresses put on it. With increased pressure, fascia hardens and tightens, creating more and larger collagen blocks and less matrix, whether the stress manifests from a physical input or emotional input. Collagen can change shape according to the pressure put upon it. Collagen can be round or block-shaped when more bonding is required. To clarify, if there is stress in the body-mind, the fascia will change from soft, flexible, and yielding to dense, thick, and gripping, making the entire body region denser, harder, and more unyielding, thus causing inflammation and pain.

Fascia's stress role coming from trauma is to protect the body from further damage. It does a great job of protecting the body by restricting movement. Where spinal disc involvement has one or more discs that bulge or herniate, the myofascial tissue on the opposing side of the spine will shorten and tighten. This neuromuscular process creates a bow-and-arrow effect that opens the vertebral spacing on the affected side. This natural process will prevent further damage to the disc or discs and nerves involved. This functional neural response is the body-mind's innate wisdom to protect the body and the species. The only problem is that it takes fascia and muscle a long time to "let go" and allow the body to resume normal strength and flexibility. Relenting fascial tension is a massive problem for people in their recovery.

Let's go back to when my back went out at age twenty-one. My fascial tissue responded to physical and emotional stress that it recalled from thirteen years earlier as a child going through similar physical and emotional stress. We now call this phenomenon myofascial tissue memory. (Myo means "muscle.") What follows is how the body-mind responds to an episode of back trauma. Lightheartedly, I referred to this body-mind process as "the issue is in the tissue."

The body-mind's reaction to stress, both emotional and physical, produces an extra tissue thickness and density where the focus resides. Understanding this complex physiological process is not essential, but knowing that this process does take place is necessary. This thickening will eventually lead to pain, inflammation, movement restriction, imbalance, and stagnation of body fluids, such as lymph and blood.

The body-mind reacts to stress in the same way an ACE bandage or brace secures a weak, painful joint. It binds the stressed region of the body together, preventing any further movement damage. Thus, connective tissue (fascia) preserves life, shapes the body, and determines its movement.

The binding tissue memory can remain in the body for years after. We initially feel better for days or weeks after a back episode, and we think we are out of the woods. Remember the body-mind has tissue memory that reactivates under the right circumstances, especially during constant chronic stress. Unfortunately, in today's hectic world, the focus is on immediate alleviation with pills or shots and not addressing a full resolution and long-term maintenance. Pain pills do work effectively, especially in the initial stages of back pain. In the case of acute and subacute pain, they are essential. They will stop the cycle of pain. Pain pills, muscle relaxers, and anti-inflammatories will reduce the pain, relax the muscles, and reduce swelling. They are essential in the initial stages of back pain, but you will find that there is much more to do to restore and maintain myofascial normalcy as you read further. And let us always be aware that complete healing requires resolving the persistent emotional components of back pain. Remember tissue memory remains to wait for another day to strike.

To summarize, stress-related back trauma episodes will activate the body-mind healing process, creating a binding of fascial tissues. The failure to resolve all stress-related factors will continue this condition. The thick fascial tissue creates a pulling and distortions on the blood vessels, nerves, muscles, joints, and bones in that region. The body-mind will always remember the affected body section of protective fascial tissue as an area with tissue trauma and weakness. Dysfunction ultimately sets in. Any stress-related-traumas that come along in the future will almost always go to the area of weakness (tissue memory).

CHAPTER 3
MANAGING YOUR BACK PAIN

Managing your back pain will begin with your first conscious recognition of back pain, whether this is your first, second, or twentieth episode. Sufferers will initially experience an uncomfortable tightness in their lower or midback, which will not stop them from doing their everyday routines. The tightness and mild pain will eventually go away. A smaller population will initially experience acute, severe pain, especially if they have had a traumatic physical trauma.

Back pain management begins with the discussion of a correct course of treatment. The stage of pain you are in will determine what practical approach you will need to take. There are three stages of back pain: acute, subacute, and chronic. These stages to the layperson can be indistinguishable because pain is not perceived the same by all and because the time spacing between the three stages can be vague. Some people think of the three stages as a chronological pattern, but that is only partially true. Pain phases will be explained in detail further on in the book. For determining what stage of pain one is in, modern medicine is guided by two factors: intensity and quality.

The medical determination for evaluating pain intensity is based on a numerical scale of one to ten (one being no pain and ten being extreme pain). The quality of pain refers to how it feels to the person. How frequently does the problem come? How long does it stay? Does it move around, or does it stay in one place? Does the pain refer to some other area of the body and is it dull, throbbing, or sharp? Note here that back pain levels will naturally increase at night and in the early morning.

Acute back pain on a numerical scale is from level seven to ten. Acute pain is sharp, constant, debilitating, and local. Acute pain can also refer to other areas of the body, causing numbness and tingling. The affected muscles are locked in and hold tightly to protect tendons, ligaments, and bones from further damage.

Subacute pain typically follows acute pain with proper care and rest. Subacute back pain levels are generally from level four to six and can still feel sharp but will come and go at intervals. The pain can be dull, throbbing, and moving but is not debilitating. As will be discussed later, subacute pain can quickly revert to acute if you are not careful in your self-care.

Chronic back pain levels generally range from one to three. In this stage, pain is no longer sharp or throbbing. The pain will be more of a dull and intermittent quality. You feel tightness, pulling, and heaviness that restrict body movement, and the pain no longer refers to other areas of the body.

A critical point to remember is there are no clear patterns and order to painful back episodes. You can experience mild level two to four pain for a while and not really be alarmed, and you will *just work through it*. Much of the time, you will recover and go back to no pain at all. However, it just takes one movement, one prolonged period of stress, and *boom!* You are no longer in mild discomfort but quickly go to acute or even the subacute stage. You can go from acute to subacute to chronic mild pain, feeling that progress is happening, and then *boom!* Right back to sharp pain again. You can also go from mild to chronic to subacute to acute.

Often there are no clear patterns or order to the coming and going of painful back episodes, and it is tough to determine your pain levels. Pain over time numbs the body and the mind. Chronically mild pain can be similar in feeling to moderate subacute pain. Even acute pain can resemble subacute pain, but to properly treat back episodes, you and your practitioner must reasonably know where you are in your pain episode. For those reasons, your health practitioner must consider other factors. Your health practitioner can determine your current stage by visual assessment, physical palpation, and asking you many questions. Knowing the stage of a back episode you are in is essential in determining the proper treatment.

Please keep in mind that sometimes even with your efforts to heal your back, you can revert to another painful episode. The culprit for these reoccurring episodes can often be attributed to an inconsistent routine of regular exercise and stretching or improper exercise and stretching. I will discuss these contributors further in the chapter called "Perpetuating Factors."

Let us now review in detail the three stages of pain and recovery.

CHAPTER 4

MANAGING YOUR BACK PAIN IN THE ACUTE STAGE

Acute stages of back pain episodes usually take three to six days for the body-mind to heal itself, reducing pain levels from a seven to ten to one to three. The typical sequence is acute to subacute to chronic. If you are still in acute pain after six days, then you must be medically diagnosed. An MRI or CAT scan will be necessary. You need to know if you have any spinal pathology.

Your body-mind works twenty-four/seven during your entire life seeking balance (homeostasis), optimal health, and a pain-free existence. There is a lot of corrective work done by your body-mind as it goes through an acute stage, so please be patient, follow the instructions, and know that recovery will occur. Know that the body-mind is correcting and working with you.

As mentioned previously, acute back pain is sharp, excruciating, localized, constant, and movement prohibitive. It can also send pain, numbness, and tingling down one or both legs. When you are in a stage of acute pain, it is critical that you immediately do the right things for yourself. The longer you delay proper self-care, the longer the recovery time and the increased possibility of creating the groundwork for a life of repetitive back pain episodes.

In essence, this is the book. Most people don't take the correct action quickly enough. They ignore the pain and live with it, believing it will magically go away and heal itself. The odd thing is that over time, it will subside to a certain degree. The problem with letting it take care of itself is that the body will never be the same as before. To clarify this complex body-mind healing process, one must understand that letting the painful condition linger and "heal itself" without proper care causes an overstimulated connective tissue response, thus causing the affected tissues to heal shorter, tighter, and thicker. You will have adhesions, imbalanced musculature, lesions, and trigger points. These physiological responses will delay or, even worse, prevent proper healing forever, leading to a life of chronic pain with repeated episodes of acute back pain. At worst, you could end up with spinal bone spurs, fractures, and scoliosis.

As stated, self-care must be an immediate action and it will be most helpful to have an aid helping you through this initial period. The first action to take is to minimalize your movements, meaning resting well supported and comfortable in bed. The bed is the place for you to rest and not in a chair or sofa. Sitting is just about the worst thing you could do for your back. Do whatever is necessary to allow yourself time to rest and heal. The only exception is to go to the bathroom. The rest period is approximately three to four days. During this rest period, you will need to determine your medical provider for evaluation and treatment. You must set up an appointment, giving yourself at least five days from the onset of pain. On average, five days will provide you with time to heal enough so that making a trip to your provider will be possible. You shouldn't drive yourself to this appointment unless your pain level is so low that you can walk and sit without significant pain by the fourth day.

I must interject here the confusing array of treatment professionals that you must choose. I will try to make this an easier task for you in chapter 6. Take the time to think about and research the healing path you wish to take. It is your decision. Decide wisely.

If you miss this opportunity to rest and heal and ignore the warning signal (pain) and put more stress on traumatized tissue, the body-mind healing process will be compromised, sending you into more prolonged pain. Eventually, if you choose to ignore your acute pain, your body-mind will put out so much pain as to debilitate you, giving you no choice but to seek help and rest your body. Remember pain is your friend. It's your body-mind sending you a clear message that something is wrong and requires action.

It is OK to be taking pain reduction medication and muscle relaxers during the acute pain stage, such as natural herbs, prescribed medication (already stocked in the house), or over-the-counter medication. Know that calling a medical doctor for pain pills won't work, for they need to see you before prescribing.

Pain reducers and muscle relaxers will work synergistically with your body-mind. I can't emphasize enough the importance of quick action, complete rest, and ice. Let your mind and body be still and quiet. Remove any influences that will arouse, disturb, excite, or depress you. Get out of bed just to go to the bathroom: no sitting at the table, no sitting watching TV, and no driving. Again, seek and *get help*.

Here are the guiding points to remember in acute pain:

- RICE: Rest and ice. Apply ice ten minutes on and ten minutes off each hour for the first seventy-two hours. Medical grade ice packs are available in stores and online. In case you don't have an ice pack, frozen peas, frozen corn, and frozen meats work well temporarily. Never directly put an ice pack onto your skin unless the ice pack utilizes a cloth covering. Using a thin towel or pillowcase will do.

- Caregiver: You'll need help. When you're in pain and injured, you can't think clearly for yourself. It is wise to ask for help, be it your spouse, offspring, neighbor, or friend. If it's possible, do not go it alone. Too many demands on yourself for the first three or four days will require getting in and out of bed. Trust me: you will be dropping things, and you shouldn't be picking up anything at all.

- Lifting: No lifting whatsoever. No bending. No twisting. If you are alone and have to pick something up from the floor, use some form of aid, such as a chair or countertop, so that you can end up on the floor in a kneeling position by bending your knees. Pick up the item, and again using some help, lift yourself back up using only the power of your leg muscles. This movement will be painful. I know. I have been there many times myself. Whatever you are picking up must be crucial to you; if not, just leave it there on the floor. Always breathe through any movement; do not hold your breath.

- Showers/baths: Never while in acute back pain.

- Sleeping and resting: Lie only on your back with your hips and knees at a ninety-degree angle. You will need two or three pillows under your legs to accomplish this. No side-sleeping in acute pain. No sitting on chairs or couches.

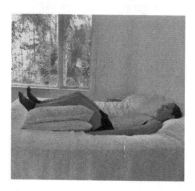

- Stretching/exercise: Absolutely no stretching or exercising is advised while in acute pain. The temptation will be there for you to self-evaluate your flexibility and pain by stretching. You must avoid this temptation because your muscles are holding you in a protective pattern. They are short and tight for a reason and will instantly go into spasm if asked to perform. They need to slowly and naturally return to normal tone over days of rest and care. In some instances, activating guarded back muscles while protecting herniated discs can cause even more nerve damage.

• Getting into bed: To enter a bed correctly so that you don't further damage your back, first choose the side of the bed you will lie on. You will lie on the side that allows you to enter and leave the bed on the shortest side of your back. You will be leaning toward the short side when standing. Knowing now what side of the bed you will lie on, you can choose two methods for entering the bed. Use the way that is easiest for you and that causes the least amount of discomfort.

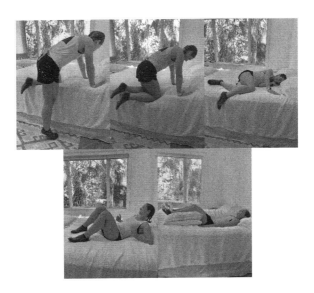

Method 1: Facing the bedside, lift one leg at a time onto the bed so that you end up on both knees and hands. You can now gently fall onto the short side of your back and then roll flat on your back. Rest your legs on at least two pillows. This

support will provide tractional relief. You can also use method 1 starting at the foot of the bed.

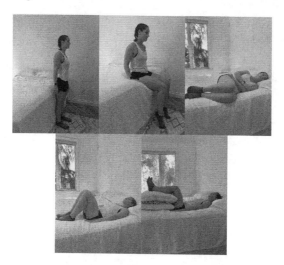

Method 2: Standing with the back of your legs against the mattress, gently sit down on the bed. Check to see that your head pillow is in the right place and gently, in one continuous motion, fall onto your side while at the same time lifting your legs onto the bed. From this position, roll onto your back and put two to three pillows under your legs for support. Choose the one method that is easiest with the least amount of pain.

- Getting out of bed: Put your legs out over the edge of the bed after rolling onto your side. Push yourself up with the arm closest to the mattress. The weight of your legs, combined with the push of your arms, will act as a fulcrum to lift you into a sitting position. Complete this motion in one gentle motion. From this sitting position, lean forward to stand entirely on your feet with knees slightly bent. Now use your large leg muscles (quadriceps and hamstrings) to come to an upright posture. You will not be able to stand fully erect, and don't attempt to because your back muscles will not allow this to happen. Don't be fearful as your back heals. You will eventually be able to stand more erect with less pain. If this method is too painful, try the following. From your back-lying position, roll onto your stomach and swivel your legs off the bed. Stand with knees almost entirely bent to reduce the strain on your back muscles. Slowly, while holding onto the bed, lower yourself onto both knees.

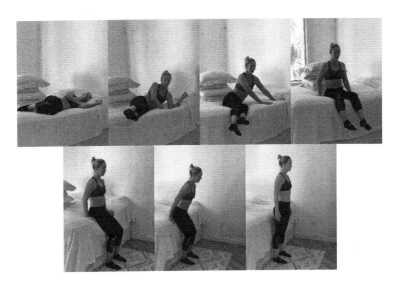

- Going to the toilet: Follow the above guides to get out of and back into bed. Out of bed and standing next to the bed, try to do a slow shuffle walk to the toilet. Normal cadence will be painful because the action of lifting your feet as you walk requires much demand from your leg and back muscles. If you can, continue to slowly shuffle walk, but if the pain is too much, then gently and slowly drop onto your knees while holding onto the mattress or some other stationary object for support. Crawl (yes, that's right) to the toilet. I have been there often because the pain from standing and walking in acute stages is almost impossible to bear. There is no self-judgment here or pity. You are using common sense, respecting the pain.

For men and women both, whether urinating or moving your bowels, sit down on the toilet bowl. Men, the worst thing you can do for your back is to ask it to hold you upright while you urinate. You are in terrible pain, and your muscles are locked in to protect the spine, discs, and nerves, so why ask them to do anything else? Once the lid is up, keep it up so that you don't have to repeat this painful procedure. The hardest thing to do and the most dangerous thing is to twist your back to reach the toilet paper holder. Have the toilet paper in front of you if you can, on a small table. Not on the floor.

Going to the toilet walking: Hold the sink counter or some other form of support and turn so that the bowl is behind you. Lower your body slowly while still holding onto the countertop. Slowly lower yourself to a sitting position. Use your leg muscles to prevent sitting too quickly. To facilitate a return to standing, push off from your knees with your hands and remember to use your leg muscles and not your back muscles.

Going to the toilet crawling: While on your knees, put both arms on the seat and then, with one arm on the seat, reach with the other arm for the countertop. Next, bring the knee closest to the counter up so that the foot is flat on the floor. Using the strength of your arms while holding onto the countertop, lift to standing, and while still supported by the countertop, turn your body so that you can sit down. To lift off the seat and return to crawling, just reverse the procedure.

- Sexual activities: Absolutely no sexual activity is advised while in the acute pain phase.

- Depression: This is a common reaction when you are incapacitated. Do your best to keep positive, knowing that this phase is temporary and healing is a continuous process. Being depressed, angry, or fearful will just lengthen your recovery time.

- Make that appointment to see your medical professional. Make it for the fifth day from the onset of your acute pain. You can always reschedule if needed.

CHAPTER 5
MANAGING YOUR BACK PAIN IN THE SUBACUTE STAGE

The subacute back pain stage usually starts by the third or fourth day of proper bed rest following the acute stage. Subacute back pain will generally reduce to a level of around four to six. Once again, try not to confuse pain level stages by its frequency but by its numerical pain value. You are still very sore and limited in movement, but you feel that you are getting better for the first time. You still have moderate tightness and painful points. Your muscles are still holding short and tight to protect but not as severe as before. They will now begin to lengthen and release. Your pain is not as consistent as before, as it will come and go. The pain might still be sharp at times but is now more pulsing and moving. You still may experience pain and/or numbness shooting down one or both legs.

Your body is processing the injury and trying to correct it. It's time now to take a look at your situation. You're still deep in the woods, and now is not the time to go back to work or to resume daily activities. You are in the critical phase where most people make the mistake of thinking, *I've made it! It's over!* It is vital now to still maintain bed rest. You will most likely be ready to see your medical practitioner now.

You will be anxious to get up and go, but don't. You should feel better knowing you can get up to use the toilet with much less pain and not have to shuffle your feet. You can take a shower now, but no bathtub. Don't sit up in bed to eat since your bed lacks the proper support but eat at the table while sitting on a supportive chair. Bed rest is necessary with legs supported so that hips and knees are at a ninety-degree angle.

Now is the time to begin your at-home rehabilitation. At-home rehabilitation should always use gentle movement exercises while lying in bed. You may now begin to exercise the mid to lower back. (Instructions to follow.)

Here are the guidelines to remember while in subacute pain:

- How to get in and out of the automobile: You are *not* to drive yourself. You are in subacute pain, and you really must have someone else drive you. There are three reasons for not driving yourself. One reason is that sitting without moving will more than likely lock up your back in spasms and you will not be able to stand upright once you arrive at your destination. The second reason is that your right foot reflexes will be diminished, causing a slow braking response. The third reason is that pain medication and muscle relaxers will make you drowsy. You should only be going to see your chosen health care professional for an appointment. There is no other reason at this point to go anywhere else. It is noteworthy to state that an SUV is preferable to a sedan or coupe because the higher seats make it easier to get in and out of the automobile. If the seat has a lumbar support function, use it so that you feel the lumbar cushion pressing gently on your lower spine. Your knees ideally should be slightly higher than your hips. While in a subacute phase of pain, don't sit for more than twenty minutes at a time. Make sure to get out of the car every twenty minutes to walk a few steps before getting back in.

- When entering the vehicle, your back goes in first. Begin by standing with the car door opened and the back legs facing in. Next, sit down and grab the steering wheel; slowly swing your body and legs into the vehicle in one motion.

- Exit the vehicle by using the security grab bar for leverage and gently swing your body and legs together outside of the car in one slow movement. Stand and close the door.

- Sitting: The correct sitting posture requires your feet to be flat on the floor with your knees bent at ninety degrees and your upper legs at ninety degrees to your hips. A pillow or cushion should support your back. Your head shouldn't be forward in front of or over your chest. After recovering from the acute and subacute pain stages, try not to sit for more than twenty minutes at a time. You need to get out of the car and walk, if only for a few minutes. This habit will keep your back from locking up and becoming stiff again. Repeated and prolonged sitting could easily take you right back into the acute or subacute pain again. Once you are pain free, you can resume your normal sitting activities, but keep in mind that prolonged sitting isn't good for your back in any condition.

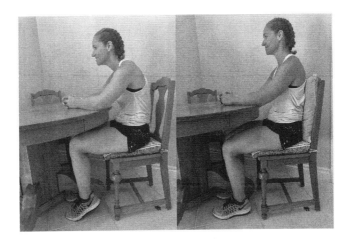

- Getting in and out of bed: refer to the acute pain guide.

- Putting on pants: First, preferably have your helper lay out on the bed the clothes you're going to wear. The fewer pieces of clothing, the better for you, so if you can do without underwear, then leave it out. This also applies to socks. Socks especially are difficult and painful to put on. Pants again are difficult and painful to put on. If pants are a must, slip your legs into them while sitting on the edge of the bed. An option is to put on the pants while lying on your back. Before putting on the pants, put on the shirt or blouse. Finally, put your shoes on while sitting in a chair. If you have a helper, let them put your shoes on for you. If possible, do not wear laced shoes but wear slip-on loafers (no flip-flops). If you must lace your shoes, then do so while sitting in a chair. To sit back up after tying your laces, use your hands on your knees to push yourself back up.

- Putting on a dress: First, preferably have your helper lay out on the bed the clothes you're going to wear. The fewer pieces of clothing, the better for you, so if you can do without underwear, leave it out. This also applies to socks. Socks especially are difficult and painful to put on. Wear a loose dress if the weather allows. Sitting on the bed's edge, slip the dress over your head. It's important that your feet touch the floor, which will provide stability. Let the dress fall so that it touches the bed. Stand by leaning forward, letting your momentum carry you to upright position. Knees are initially bent until fully upright, then straighten your legs. Finally, put your shoes on while sitting in a chair. If you have a helper, let them put your shoes on for you. If possible, do not wear laced shoes but wear slip-on loafers (no flip-flops). If you must lace your shoes, then do so while sitting in a chair. To sit back up after tying your laces, use your hands on your knees to push yourself back up.

- How to shave at the sink: You shouldn't shave at all until you are in a mild chronic stage of pain, but if you must shave, then use a washcloth to heat and moisten your face as well as to clean off the shaving cream. Do not bend over the sink as this could cause your back muscles to spasm and lock.

- Ice or heat: When you are in subacute pain, apply only heat. Ten minutes on and twenty minutes off each hour, as is necessary. Alternate heat with ice only if the pain increases. If the pain becomes acute, then go back to the previous guide for acute pain.

- Going to the toilet: You should be able when you are in subacute pain to use the bathroom as you usually would just use the sink counter to lower and raise yourself from the bowl. If needed, refer to the acute instructions. Remember to keep the toilet paper in front of you, not to twist to reach for it.

- Sexual activity: prohibitive in subacute pain.

- Depression: refer to the acute pain guide.

- Daily hygiene: No baths, but quick showers are possible. Liquid soap is preferable to a soap bar, which can slip from your hands, meaning that you will have to bend to pick it up. Dry your legs and feet while in a sitting position with the leg to be dried crossed over the other leg's knee.

- Keep stress levels low. Avoid stress-inducing TV shows and worrying about money, jobs, and family. This is not the time to find faults and blame either yourself or others. And this is not the time for arguments with anyone.

- Gentle movement exercises: As long as your pain is mild to moderate, you can begin to introduce gentle movement exercises into your recovery. Remember if any movement increases pain, stop immediately.

- Pelvic tilts: To do this correctly, you're in a back-lying position with your legs supported by pillows. While gently inhaling, tilt your pubic bone up toward your head and simultaneously tighten your abdominal muscles, bringing your belly button down toward your spine. Do not push with your feet. Use only the abdominal and back muscles in this movement. Exhaling, let your pelvis gently rock back by gently pressing the sacrum into the bed, breathing normally. If this movement causes pain, then tilt even more gently, more slowly, and with less range of motion. If this movement still brings on pain, stop the exercise altogether. Repeat this exercise for five repetitions. You can repeat this exercise hourly so long as you have no discomfort during or after.

- Knees to chest: To do this correctly, you're in a back-lying position with your legs supported by pillows. Bring one knee at a time up toward the same side shoulder. With both hands holding your knee on each side, inhale, and as you exhale, *gently* bring that knee up toward the shoulder. No pulling! Just bring the knee up to the point where there is *no pain,* and you begin to feel a slight resistance. Repeat five times, with each knee always working with the breath. If no pain, you can repeat this exercise hourly.

- Hamstring stretch: Lying on your back, lift the active leg to hold it just above the knee. The leg needs to be straight. The resting leg can be bent at a slight angle to ease the back. Pain shouldn't be present. You should only feel a good stretch. While holding the leg, let the knee bend and then straighten the leg again. Hold the stretch for three seconds, and repeat ten times. Repeat ten times with the other leg.

- Calf stretch: The starting position is the same as the hamstring stretch. While holding the straight, lifted leg at the knee, push the heel up toward the ceiling. Hold the stretch for three seconds, and repeat ten times. Repeat ten times with the other leg.

- Gentle rocking: Lying on your back, bring both knees up so that your feet are lying on the bed. Put a pillow or cushion between your legs. Now very gently begin to roll your bent legs from side to side. If you feel pain, you are rocking too vigorously, too quickly, and you need to decrease the range of motion and slow down the pace. Only rock within the rhythm of your normal breath. Do not cross one leg over the other. By doing so, you can overstretch your muscles.

CHAPTER 6

MANAGING YOUR BACK PAIN IN THE CHRONIC STAGE

It is important not to think of chronic pain as a chronological order of time, meaning reoccurring episodes over time, but as a pain level. I am addressing here only your pain level and not the frequency of occurrences. Some people go through most of their lives with frequent reoccurring chronic back pain episodes, while some have very few.

Chronic back pain episodes fall within pain levels, with levels one to three being mild. Flexibility and muscle strength should be good so that through your self-care, you will continue to improve. If this is your first time experiencing mild back pain, carry on with your everyday life activities, but be cautious because mildly chronic back pain still means something is not right down there.

OK, now you know your back has spoken up, and it's told you something down there isn't quite right. Your back has said to you, "Pay attention, or you will go down." You need to see your health care practitioner. You are on the road to recovery. Even for those experiencing just mild back pain for the first time, this chapter is also for you. Everyone needs to take back pain seriously. A mildly tweaked back with pain level can elevate to a level ten quickly if not heeded. Your flexibility and muscle strength will directly correspond to your level of back pain.

By now, four to seven days of bed rest has occurred, and your back pain is around a level one to three. You are feeling optimistic that you will be normal again and pain free. Your body feels like it can get up and move around, but only do this *slowly and carefully*. The pain you feel is no longer sharp, throbbing, stabbing, or pulsing. Pain no longer stays in one area but is spread out, covering one or more body regions. Your flexibility and strength are improving, allowing movement to be quicker and less painful. You can also breathe more comfortably and more naturally.

You should no longer have pain, tingling, or numbness shooting down your leg at this point. If you still do, there is the possibility you may have spinal disc pathology, and you must see a medical practitioner for an accurate diagnose using body scans, MRIs, or x-rays. In addition to seeing a medical doctor or a chiropractor, being treated by a massage therapist, an acupuncturist, or a physical therapist would be beneficial.

If your back pain isn't interfering with your daily life, continue with your daily activities, but be on guard for any movement that could throw your back into spasm. It is vital to be active again once your pain levels are mild. Your body-mind needs muscle demand to restore proper tissue memory. Continuous bed rest is not only unnecessary at this point but could be a hindrance to your continued improvement. Now is the time to add more gentle movement exercises to your daily routine, but again, keep in mind the golden rule that pain induced by exercise means you have moved too fast and too far. Just be careful.

You are at a vitally important fork in the road. Just one wrong move or extended period of stress can put you back into an acute phase again. Be very careful, aware, and conscientious.

Do your best to be calm, keeping stressful thoughts and circumstances at a minimum. It's a good time for self-reflection, focusing on what you have gained with this back pain occurrence. Reflect on your circumstances and ask, "Are they purely physical, or are there possible emotional attachments to it?"

Self-care guides while in the chronic stage of mild back pain include the following:

- Ice/heat: A long shower or bath in the morning will loosen up your back. Soaking in a tub with the combination of Epsom salts and the essential oils of peppermint and rosemary will help to reduce your pain, relax you, and detox your muscles. Once your pain level is stable at levels one to three, it will be time to apply a combination of ice and heat. You use ice for five minutes and then heat for ten minutes, altering for one hour, and then wait an hour before applying again. The ice/heat combo will decrease the inflammation and increase blood flow to the injury site. The blood flow is essential to healing as it provides nutrition and promotes cell waste disposal.

- Sports: No high-stress impact sporting activities, such as golf, tennis, running, jogging, and CrossFit training, are beneficial while you are in mild chronic back pain. You will more than likely aggravate your condition by going back too fast. Your health care provider will guide you as to when you can resume sporting activities.

- Professional help: You have choices to make now. If you are seeing a medical doctor or chiropractor, you can stay with them exclusively. They will recommend seeing a physical therapist or an athletic trainer to further your recovery. You can also choose to see an alternative health care provider alone or adjunct to your medical doctors, such as an acupuncturist and a massage therapist. All choices are good and will speed up your recovery.

- Lifting: You need to be extra careful when lifting objects regardless of their weight. The most dangerous way to lift is bending from the waist with straight legs or even slightly bent knees. The safest, most efficient way to lift is to use the power of your legs' muscles. This means bending your knees until you can securely grip the object. You must keep your back straight and tighten your abdominal muscles while lifting. Once lifted, hold the object above the waist and close to the body. Never lift an object unless it is in front of you and not to the side. Correct lifting needs to remain a lifelong habit.

- Sitting: refer to the subacute guide.

- Getting in and out of the car: refer to the subacute pain guide.

- Sink activities: When washing your face or removing shaving cream at a sink, lower yourself by bending your knees and not bending from your waist. Resting on your forearms will take the pressure off of your back. This is good advice to use throughout your life.

- Shoes: Until you are entirely out of the woods, wear easy to slip into shoes that don't require lacing. Once you are pain free, you can go back to laced shoes. Do not wear flip-flops (actually never wear flip-flops); they do not support proper spine alignment, nor do they support walking or standing.

- Sleeping: Still try to sleep on your back at night with your legs supported. Back sleeping is always preferred for back health. If you want to try side sleeping, now you are ready. If it bothers you, stop immediately. Sleep on the side of the spine that is the least painful. Sleep closer to the edge to make it easier to exit the bed. Sleep with a pillow between your knees, a pillow against your chest, a pillow against the back, and a small pillow to lay under the upper arm. Be sure your head is not tilted either up or down.

- Getting in and out of bed: refer to the acute pain guide.

- Dishwasher: Always lift your back foot to take the pressure off of your back. Don't just bend forward from the waist with straight legs together.

- Add gentle movement exercises.

    Even with mild back pain, you must still be careful not to overstretch or overwork the back muscles. Rule 1 is to not stretch a muscle beyond its range of comfort. Do not create pain while stretching. If you try to lengthen a muscle beyond its current capability, you will create a pain response. Take your muscle to the point of first pain and then back off the stretch until there is no pain at all. It is OK to feel the stretch but not to feel the pain. Rule 2 is not to hold the stretch for too long that will result in pain. I prefer a three-second stretch repeated ten times versus a thirty- to sixty-second stretch repeated just once. This is essential for muscles in recovery. Once the muscles have fully recovered, have a healthy tone, and are warmed up, you can stretch pain free anywhere from ten to sixty seconds.

These stretching rules are of my personal opinion based on my own experiences with back pain and being a certified isolated muscle stretch therapist. I advise you to follow the exercise instructions given by your health care provider. If they are not benefiting you, share your thoughts with your health care provider. In general, you need to be cautious of yoga or Pilates while in mild back pain. In my opinion, your instructor needs to specialize in rehabilitation yoga or Pilates. In my practice, I had many people come to me with elevated back pain due to overly aggressive yoga or Pilates. My opinion is to be cautious.

You can add the following exercises now to the pelvic tilting and pelvic rocking that you have been doing while in subacute pain. Using a belt, rope, or stretch band begins to stretch your calves and hamstring muscles. Wrap the band around the bottom of your foot just in front of the heel on the active leg. The inactive leg is bent at a thirty-degree angle. Now on your exhalation, raise the active leg slowly and gently until you reach that point where your leg will not go any further without inducing pain. For three seconds (count them as one thousand one, one thousand two, and one thousand three), gently put just a slightly more stretch on the leg by softly pulling on the stretch band. On your inhalation, lower your leg, and during the next exhalation, repeat the exercise nine more times. Repeat this on the other leg.

Another good exercise is to sit on a stable chair, positioning your buttocks halfway back. Slowly lean forward from the waist, letting your hands flow slowly from your thighs, over the knees, and down the shin bone as far as you can without inducing pain. Hold for three seconds and repeat five times.

Next, if you can, while standing and holding onto a stationary object like a countertop, bend the active leg behind you so you can hold your ankle. On the exhalation, press your active knee down toward the ground while pushing your hip bone out forward. Keep the abdominal muscles tight. You will feel a stretch on the quadriceps muscles of the active leg. Hold the stretch for two to three seconds while exhaling. Inhale while letting the leg go back to its normal position, and then repeat the stretch on the next exhalation. You can do five to ten repetitions.

A good hip stretch is sitting on a chair halfway to the back. Cross one leg over onto the other so that the ankle rests just above the knee. If holding this position gives you a good stretch, then go no further. Hold the stretch for two to three seconds while exhaling. Inhaling, go back to the starting position. You can do five to ten repetitions. If you feel you can stretch further, then while your leg is crossed and laying on top of the other, just lean forward ever so gently until you feel a good stretch without pain. The stretch should be felt in the buttock from the sacrum to just past the hip joint. Be careful not to overdo it on this one.

The final stretch is done again while sitting halfway on a stable chair. It is simply to rotate the upper body to each side while the legs are kept stationary. Hold each stretch two to three seconds while exhaling. Go back to the neutral forward position while inhaling. You can repeat this stretch five to ten times. Your hands can be on your knees or folded across the chest.

Traction: An excellent alternative to sitting while reading or watching TV is to lie on the floor with a traction pillow under your legs. You can buy a traction pillow online or in a retail store. If you don't have a pillow, you can lie on the floor with your lower legs resting on a chair. The idea of traction is to create more spacing between the spinal vertebrae, thus creating more blood flow and muscle toxin release.

The last words of wisdom I wish to pass on to you at this juncture in your healing is that the episodic cycles of pain can very quickly repeat over and over again. Your efforts to come to grips with the physical and emotional components will determine whether your back pain will be a lifelong experience or a few-and-far-between experience. I decided in midlife to make my changes. I decided to find my true calling and to seek my joy and release my darkness. The things that caused me the most stress I released. I chose to love my back and to do my best to help it. I searched and found many answers to my body-mind pain's physical, metaphysical, and spiritual aspects.

CHAPTER 7
PERPETUATING FACTORS

OK, so let's talk about back health once you have recovered from your last back episode. You are now feeling well again with little or no pain. You still may be in the care of a medical health care provider. You could be doing your at-home stretch routine, trying to increase your flexibility and strength. Hopefully, you are seeing a chiropractor, an acupuncturist, a massage therapist, or all of them combined. Whether this was your first occurrence or one of many or whether you suffered a mild episode or an acute episode, you will have this worrying thought: *Will this happen to me again?* This is a normal fearful thought based on what you have already encountered. Remember that you have the ability and control to minimize the reoccurrences or perhaps even prevent them from happening again. This self-empowerment emanates from knowing what factors will create the reoccurrences.

The most important thing to remember is that all of the factors discussed here can stimulate the neuromuscular pain response system into reactivation. These factors are known as perpetuating factors (PF). These are the conditions that will disrupt the body-mind balance. In no particular order of importance, I will explain these factors. Keep in mind many of these PF are your lifestyle choices and are totally within your control.

Stress

Let me begin with the perpetuating factor called stress. I described how our thought patterns' unique relationship affects our general health in previous chapters. Stress that is constant and repetitive over a considerable time will adversely affect your body's and mind's health. Fear and anger are two primary stress-related emotions that stimulate the fight-or-flight syndrome. As said previously in this book, these two emotions work well in the preservation of ourselves. Still, when unresolved and repeated over and over again, they will negatively affect our health.

These stress-related negative thought patterns will directly affect our body systems, notably the connective tissue system, the nervous system, the muscular system, the cardiovascular system, and the digestive system. On the physical aspect, unrelenting stress can literally, over time, change the shape (alignment) of our bodies. By bending and twisting our bodies out of alignment, stress will disrupt the flow of body-mind energy that will eventually lead to "dis-ease." We must be aware of stress levels in our lives and know that disease and pain will pursue when it is constant and unresolved. Be mindful of your stress factors, and seek ways to reduce or resolve them.

During my years in my practice, I have witnessed, time and again, clients complaining of repeated back pain for unknown reasons. In my assessment evaluation, I find they haven't had any major physical traumas in their lives that would have contributed to their problem. Continuing with my intake, it became apparent that they have carried an excessive amount of unresolved emotional stress in their lives and that these stresses manifested into physical pain patterns. Remember unrelenting pain caused by stress will activate the muscular/connective tissue systems to shorten and tighten in the body's regions directly related to stress.

For instance, clients with repeated or constant neck pain and stiffness usually complained of a lifetime of having to make multiple complicated choices and then having to express those choices vocally. They were fearful not only of deciding but also afraid of vocalizing that decision. They didn't know which way to turn and how to speak their thoughts, resulting in a stagnated area of blocked negative energy in the neck, throat, and arms. These neck pain sufferers also explained that they have a reluctance to speak up for themselves. Very restricted myofascial neck tissue created this block and resulting pain. A headache is a frequent symptom also resulting from this condition. Another cause of chronic neck pain for my clients was improper breathing patterns resulting from excessive anxiety. They all unconsciously breathed shallowly from their upper chests only and not using the abdomen's breathing muscles, notably the diaphragms. When they only breathed from their upper chest, they had to incorporate their neck muscles attached to their collar bones, which helped lift the upper ribs and expand the lungs upward. These same muscles also had to turn the head, hold the head up, tilt the head down, and tilt the head backward. By demanding muscles do too many functions simultaneously, longtime chronic exhaustion will occur. In this case, the neck muscles. Chronically exhausted muscles will tighten, weaken, and go into pain.

Many of my clients complained of foot, ankle, knee, and hip pain, with no apparent explanation discovered through our conversations that they were "stuck" at a juncture of their lives. For many reasons, they are unable to make necessary decisions, enabling them to move forward in life. Being "stuck" in their lives created unresolved stress that manifested itself as weakened myofascial tissue in the lower back, which in turn formed blood and nerve flow impingements to the hips and legs, thus creating joint dysfunction of the hips, knees, and feet/ankles. Our legs are our mobility to move as well as energetically our ability to move forward in life. Negative emotions such as fear will prevent our transitioning through life and lock our lower back and legs, causing pain and myofascial dysfunction.

Our bodies are organized into psychosomatic (mind-body) zones interconnected to each other physically and energetically. Mental stress will tighten and shorten the connective tissues (primarily fascia) within these zones. Not only will the connective tissue tighten within a zone restricting movement, but the zones themselves will become less movement integrated. This body-mind stress response completely disrupts the body's ability to maintain its health, move, align itself in gravity, and generally feel right.

The head is the "thinking" zone. The chest is the "being" zone. The arms and legs are the "doing" zones. The neck integrates the thinking to our "being self." The pelvis integrates the "being" to our "doing." The shoulders integrate the "being" to our "doing." When people feel they have a bad back, there is almost always a mental or emotional stressful thought pattern blocking the integration of the "being" to the doer. The result is a painful tightness in the lower back. This was also true if the initial stress was from a physical trauma accompanying negative thought patterns during the physical trauma.

It is essential in keeping a healthy back to reduce the frequency of fear/anger stress, even more so with related physical traumas. The scope of how to accomplish this is so vast as not to apply to this book's writing. There are thousands of resources available to us today to help us with our stress. Please avail yourselves to them. Get it done, and live your life with a healthier back.

Physical Traumas

The second PF is the more obvious physical traumas of life, such as falls, automobile accidents, and sports injuries. This PF is an unavoidable part of life, but I have to mention it because these physical traumas often lead to mild, moderate, or severe back pain. Often, as mentioned above, there is an attached negative thought pattern before, during, or after the physical trauma itself, and this negative thought pattern will influence the degree of severity and duration of your back pain episodes

Insufficient Sleep

This third PF is partnered directly to the first factor of stress. The current scientific thinking is seven to eight hours of sleep a night is needed for a healthy body and the brain. Our fascia, muscles, and tendons need that much time to recuperate from the day, especially during a back pain episode or in times of relentless stress. Sleep and rest are nature's medicine for the health of our whole body/mind. Try to establish a consistent habit of going to bed and getting up within a specified time frame. It's not always the easiest thing to do every day, but try your best to do so. Shut off the TV, computer, phone, and iPad at least a half hour before bedtime.

Make sure your mattress and your pillow work well together so that your body can fully relax and not have to toss and frequently turn to find a comfortable position. You may need to replace your mattress every seven years or so. When sleeping on your back, your head should not be pushed forward. The mattress should naturally support the cervical and lumbar curves of the spine. You should also have a pillow under your knees to aid back comfort. When sleeping on your side, your entire spine needs to be straight, including your sacrum. Sleeping on your stomach is not beneficial for your health. It will not support proper spinal alignment. It could also impede blood flow through the aortic artery, and it could interfere with the internal organs' natural rhythms.

Infections

The next PF is acute infections that can activate back muscle trigger points. Specific for the lower and midback are infections of the lungs, sinuses, and gut. Coughing, sneezing, and intestinal inflammation can all activate these trigger points. When sneezing, please remember that you *never* bend from your knees and lean forward but stay upright as much as you can. Sometimes a very hard sneeze can cause a spinal disc to bulge or herniate out of its boney, protective compartment.

Sports Sense

Let's talk about another PF that I call *sports sense* or, as in the case of back trauma, the lack of it. Too many people just don't know when to quit. The common thought of "no pain, no gain" is wrong for your health on so many levels. No matter what the sporting activity is, when the body cries out "Enough!" please heed the call. An exhausted muscle needs to rest to detox and replenish. The weekend warriors who are inactive during the work week then go out on the weekend and try to be Olympic athletes are vulnerable to muscle injury.

Another mistake people often make is the lack of sufficient pre- and post-activity stretching. Muscles should never be put into a high demand mode when they are cold and tight. The most common results will be muscle strains, tears, or muscle spasms with activated trigger points, and in some incidences, tendon/ligament injury could occur. Muscles need at least six to ten minutes of prewarm-up before high demand exercise. I ride a stationary bike for seven minutes to warm up, and then I stretch for another ten minutes before performing any exercise. Just as essential as the pre-activity warm-up is post-activity cooldown with stretching. The more demanding the sport or activity, the longer the pre-event warm-up stretch and post-event cooldown and stretch. There are endless forms of information on this subject for you to look up. As in any post-pain recovery case, it would be wise to consult with a sports massage therapist, a personal trainer, an athletic trainer, or a physical therapist.

Body's Structural Misalignments

A serious influencer of back pain that goes mainly unrecognized by the mainstream population is our body's structural misalignments, better known as poor posture. Body alignment refers to our bony skeletal segments' spatial and mechanical relationships and how they stack up against the downward push of gravity as we stand and move. Gravity would not be a factor if we, like other animals, stood and moved on four legs, but this is not our fate. As humans, we are unique in that we can move and stand on two legs, but by doing so, we put enormous demand on our front and back muscles. Some of our muscles are for action, and some for structural support. Some muscles do both. The former are called fast-twitch muscles, and the latter are called slow-twitch muscles. The abdominal muscles of the front and spinal erector muscles of the back are such moving structural muscles and therefore hold us up in gravity and help us bend forward and bend backward.

When our bodies are out of alignment, more onus is on these structural muscles. For example, when people have their heads hanging way forward of their chests and their upper backs bowed, the spinal support muscles front and back are overloaded and weaken. We also have seen people who tilt to one side or whose head tilts to one side. We notice some people having one shoulder higher than the other. Some others have an exaggerated curve to their lower backs with their buttocks raised. All of these postures are examples of body misalignment.

Knowing the physiological processes that go into creating body misalignments are not essential to the writing of this book (it would fill an entire book by itself), but what is critical is knowing body misalignments will create the following conditions:

- blocked flows of life energy
- painful movement compensations through inarticulations of the joints, thus interfering with the ease of movement
- pain from overly demanded muscles, commonly the muscles of the neck and back
- impeded flow of blood, lymph, nerves, spinal fluid, and oxygen
- interference with rhythms innervating the body's organs

In general, body misalignments can distort the spine's structure, which will affect the flow of nerve communication throughout the entire body, leading to a plethora of possible ill health.

Where the spinal bones bend, twist, and extend out of their proper alignment, there can be nerve impingements on the spinal nerves. These spinal distortions are called subluxations. A subluxation is a misalignment or loss of normal movement of one of the bones in your spine. Subluxated spinal bones lacking in movement will cause faster than normal wear and tear in the surrounding muscles and discs, resulting in pain, inflammation, and degeneration. The sciatic nerve is the most common nerve impingement affecting the back, hips, and legs.

Body misalignments can be changed and corrected in many different ways. In general, the younger the body, the easier and quicker it is to correct misalignments. There are two reasons for this. The younger tissue is softer, more pliant, and healthier than older tissue. The second reason is that misalignments in a younger body haven't had enough time to set up tissue dysfunction. The older the body, the more it is settled in its alignment, and the more difficult it is to change. Remember me saying the body's connective tissue by nature is plastic, meaning it can change shape and structure, but as we age, connective tissue dries and it is harder for it to change.

In no order of importance, the following practices can help with body alignment: a certified myofascial structural integrative bodyworker, a certified neuromuscular massage therapist, an acupuncturist, an orthopedic surgeon, chiropractic, and a physical therapist. Several nonmedical practices will also help realign the body. The best-known practices are Pilates, yoga, Tai Chi, Qigong, and Egoscue. It is my opinion that not one of these practices is complete in and of itself. My advice is to integrate these practices. An important starting place is with a certified myofascial structural integrative bodyworker/massage therapist. Their specific skills focus directly on the realignment of the myoskeletal organization. I have used many of the practices mentioned above to rehabilitate my back. I have had countless sessions with myofascial structural integrative bodyworkers and acupuncturists. I have been going to chiropractors for forty-eight years and physical therapy in the most recent years. Over time I have practiced Pilates, yoga, Tai Chi, and Qigong, all with excellent results. Body health is not a one-and-done thing. It is a lifetime commitment.

Note: By Florida law, a chiropractor needs one hundred hours of education in acupuncture to hold that certification, and an MD needs zero hours. A licensed acupuncturist needs 3,000 hours to have that degree.

Incorrect Ergonomics

By now, most of us have heard about incorrect ergonomics and how that contributes to body pain. Still, it needs further discussion, for it is too essential a perpetuating factor when it comes to originating and continuing back pain. Body misalignments can be created by and remain through improper ergonomics. Wrongful sitting, which involves how long one sits and the way one sits, is the most evident PF for neck and back pain. Modern-day living and technology have created a human condition called "forward-flexed" bodies. This means we spend our lives sitting so much and so improperly to cause our bodies to fold into a forward position. The advent of computer screens, TVs, cell phones, laptops, iPads, workstations, and automobiles have kept us in a folded-in sitting posture with a head-forward posture and rounded backs. Whether at home eating dinner or watching TV, in school at our desk, at work in front of a computer, or in our car, we find ourselves sitting, sitting, sitting.

Let's face it: we spend most of our lives either lying flat in bed or sitting. For the most part, we no longer till the fields, work in the factory, or construct the roads. We sit. Our bodies are becoming shorter in front and longer in the back, which is an easy thing for the body to do since this posture is natural for the first nine months of living in gestation. This forward, folded body alignment makes it hard for humans to stand upright correctly. It takes months for a newborn baby to learn how to walk upright in gravity. Being forward, flexed creates a shorter and tighter front line of connective tissue (fascia and muscle). The opposing backline is more elongate and weaker. This constant pulling forward force is a perpetual strain on our back, which is exhausted trying to keep us erect.

Since excessive sitting is the culprit, we need to lessen its adverse effects by alerting ourselves to our sitting posture. Our feet need to be flat on the floor with the knees bent at ninety degrees and hips at ninety degrees. Our shoulders need to be relaxed and dropped down with our elbows at a ninety-degree angle. The shoulders should line up with the ears, and the chin needs to be neither tilted up or down. This ideal sitting position is directly related to the ratio aspect of table height to chair height. Your computer monitor height needs to be such that your head doesn't come forward and your chin is in the neutral position. Your back should be supported by the chair back, and if your back doesn't reach the chair back, you need to put a pillow or cushion there to support the lumbar spine. The chair's height has to be such that your feet are solidly on the floor and your hips and knees are at a ninety-degree angle. And lastly, try to remember not to sit for longer than thirty minutes at a time. I know this is hard to do, but try to make it a habit. You need to stand up and gently bend backward with your hands behind your back. Gentle side-to-side twisting and walking are also beneficial for your neck and back. These simple movements will break the muscle/fascia memory of a shortened and tightened forward body/head.

Not many auto manufacturers go all out on providing highly comfortable, ergonomic front car seats. This goes for most automobiles unless they are in the near-luxury or luxury status. Most car seats are, at best, just mildly supportive for the body. The correct sitting position has your knees at or slightly higher than your hips, your shoulders dropped and relaxed, your thighs supported, and your ribs supported, and you should be slightly reclined. If you are the driver, all of the above is true, and your arms should be slightly forward of your chest. Your shoulders should line up with your ears. If your car seats don't accommodate the above ergonomics, you can find excellent car seat cushions in stores and online that will help support your back. Excessive sitting will cause muscle fatigue, stiffness, and pain. When this happens, make sure to get out of the car and move about by walking and stretching. Especially true when recovering from a painful back episode. When I was recovering from acute back pain, I would get out of the car every twenty minutes. Stopping often to move about inconvenienced me, but it did make a difference.

Weather Conditions

I had to add this PF because weather conditions can affect your back. This PF came to mind just as I am writing this chapter. I am currently experiencing a cold snap in Florida, where it will go down to thirty-one degrees tonight, and my back hurts more than usual. It is incredible how I can experience back pain and not give it a thought. But I do know that cold, damp weather creates blood stasis. Blood stasis is a bodily condition whereby blood stagnates and moves sluggishly through the tissues and cells, in particular muscles superficially close to the skin. These nutritionally depleted muscles will then tighten and go into pain. Always take extra precaution when old man winter breathes its cold air upon you.

So slow down, dress warmly, and know that your back muscles will not have their regular supply of heated blood during this time. At this time, a simple movement like picking up a fallen garbage can throw your back out for days. It happened to me. How many times have you heard about shoveling snow that has thrown out people's backs? If you are thinking about working your body physically during cold, damp weather, I would advise warming up beforehand with simple movements like walking in place, side-to-side twisting, shoulder rolls, and side-to-side bending. It's imperative, even more so now, to use your legs and not your back when bending over.

Suppose you do happen to hurt your back while in cold weather. Go back to basics and ask yourself if your condition is acute, subacute, or mildly chronic, and then take the proper steps necessary. I would recommend that if your back pain results from cold, damp weather and is only mild, apply heat to the affected area for ten minutes. Repeat as often as you need. Also, you can supplement with natural or prescribed muscle relaxers.

Another weather PF is barometric pressure. In periods of low pressure, there will be a reversal of forces from inside the body to outside the body, causing more pain. You can't avoid this condition or do much about it other than rest more and take natural or pharmaceutical muscle relaxers.

Lack of Exercise

The optimal health of the human body requires it to move. The human body wasn't designed by nature to be static. Muscles with a healthy tone need demands put on them. Unhealthy muscles are either hypertonic or hypotonic. The former tone is overly tight, and the latter tone is excessively lax. A healthy muscle needs to expand and contract with equal force, eliminating tightness and laxity. Full-movement exercises like walking, swimming, jogging, yoga, and Pilates are optimal for muscle health.

Adversely, inactivity will tighten, shorten, and weaken a muscle. This condition is called muscular atrophy. It is vital when recovering from a bout of muscle pain to put demands on those affected muscles to restore capable muscle memory. The worst thing to do after recovery is to do nothing at all. Move it, or lose it!

Repetitive Motion Injury

Repetitive motion is the continuous directional force demand put on a muscles over time. A clear example is the overly tight pectoralis muscles of a person who works on a computer five days a week, fifty weeks a year. Sitting with the arms forward on a desk will fold the chest in, round the upper back, bring the head forward, and round the shoulders inward. The excessive tightness of the chest-to-arm muscles (pectoralis) will cause the upper back muscles to exhaust and weaken, causing shoulder joint inarticulation, which leads to shoulder joint bursitis tendonitis (rotator tears). Repetitive motion muscle stress does not always involve movement; it can also occur in a static posture. Sitting in a forward-leaning posture will overly shorten the front abdominal muscles, putting excessive stress on the mid/lower back muscles that continuously contract to bring the chest and head up. It is clear that after years of this repetitive motion, the back will weaken to the point where it just goes out.

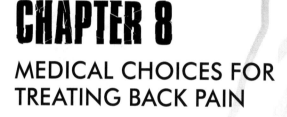

CHAPTER 8

MEDICAL CHOICES FOR TREATING BACK PAIN

Your choice of health care providers and subsequent treatments must be made wisely, for these decisions will directly affect how you heal. Be aware that you may be in so much pain that clear and focused thinking can be hampered. You may want to seek the trusted help of a family member or friend. Hopefully, the pursuing guide will provide you with enough valuable information to make your health decisions more enduring. It is up to you to decide which course of action you wish to take. Before you consider your medical direction, you must first consider several criteria that will affect your decision. Let's begin with your finances.

The reality is that often medical choices may come down to your finances and whether or not you can afford that route. One of today's frustrating conditions as it pertains to medical expenses is that private and governmental insurance plans will, in general, only cover medical bills from an allopathic doctor or chiropractic physician. For the most part, complementary and alternative medicines are paid out of pocket; thus, who and what your insurance carrier will cover could be your first decision-making criterion. Your insurance policy will often dictate who you can see, how often, what is covered, how much they will pay, and how much you will pay for deductibles and copay. Employers' workman's compensation insurance plans will take effect only if your back is injured while performing your work responsibilities. Workman's compensation insurance is definite about who your provider is, what treatments will be covered, and how frequent and how many visits you will have.

Do not visit a medical provider if you are in acute pain. Ideally, see your medical provider while in the end stages of subacute pain or the chronic stage. If prolonged sitting or standing still bother your back, do not see a medical provider. You must schedule your first appointment as soon as possible during the early phase of acute pain. You can always reschedule if you are not able to go.

Another criterion when seeking medical help is one's own beliefs and knowledge of the healing fields. Some people will tend to lean toward Western medical doctors, and others will tend to seek out more holistic, alternative, and complementary medical practices. Any decision you make will be right as long as you get the positive results you need. Understanding what to expect from the various healing fields will give you a clearer picture of your options. Each profession evaluates and treats pain differently. It is wise to be sure that your chosen health care provider has the knowledge, skills, and experience specific to treating back pain.

You will want to be assured that your health care provider's reputation, skills, and effectiveness are of the highest standards. There are three means of finding the above criteria. The first is to go online to the US State's Department web site for licensed medical discipline and regulations. All states have a department of regulation for health care professions. You can go online to these specific departments to review a provider's background, education, and legal infractions, if any. Next, you can go online to the medical provider's web site that details the provider's bio, education, skills, etc. and have patient testimonials and reviews. Lastly, there are reliable word-of-mouth referrals from friends and family. Listed below are the most prevalent health care professions that people seek. There are three distinct categories according to their approach to diagnosis and treatment.

Allopathic Medicine

In this medical field, also known as Western medicine, you will find medical doctors (MDs) and doctors of osteopathy (DOs). In general, allopathic diagnostics will incorporate a health history, an objective/subjective symptom evaluation, evaluation of x-rays, body scans, and MRIs. Allopathic doctors can prescribe pharmaceuticals drugs, possible surgery, physical therapy, bioelectric modalities, and injections. Allopathic medicine has its origins in nineteenth-century Europe and North America.

Physical therapists will fall into this group as adjuncts. Physical therapists reestablish muscle/joint function and proper body mechanics by using strengthening and stretching exercises and are limited in practice to manual, mechanical, and electrical therapies. If the treatments are billable through insurance, physical therapists must follow the prescribed codes. Also falling into the allopathic context are pharmacists, who fill prescriptions ordered by physicians.

Many back pain sufferers opt to see their primary doctor first. This may not be such a good option. Most primary physicians do not specialize in back pain, and they are overwhelmed with a large patient load. They will most likely refer you to a specialist, such as an orthopedist or a physiatrist. They can't prescribe muscle relaxers or pain pills without a physical exam.

Alternative Medicine

There are licensed .health care professionals, such as chiropractors, acupuncturists (doctors of Oriental medicine), and massage therapists, in the branch of medicine. Homeopaths and naturopaths also fall into this medical field but are not licensed. They are not licensed but have absolutely no reflection on their skills and abilities as health care providers. They do have to be certified, which requires substantial educational hours. Alternative medicine is a body of health care focusing more on the body's natural healing ability and patient participation. Alternative medicine practitioners can diagnose radiology reports, body scans, and blood work and prescribe natural herbs, supplements, and manual/hands-on therapies; however, they can't prescribe pharmaceutical drugs.

Acupuncturists, also known as doctors of Oriental medicine, rely more on an all-encompassing medical intake and health history to diagnose. They will spend a good deal of time listening to you in a detailed face-to-face interview. They also will use tongue and pulse diagnostics to understand your medical conditions fully. Acupuncturists in the United States most commonly practice TCM (traditional Chinese medicine), which is an ancient practice. Acupuncturists have many therapies at their disposal, the most common being herbal supplements, needling, moxibustion, ear seeds, electrostimulation, acupressure, tui-na massage, shiatsu, cupping, and qua sha.

Massage therapists are not allowed by law to diagnose health conditions, but they can assess and treat as it applies to soft tissue. Massage therapist assessments and treatments rely heavily on a detailed client health history report, a pain location model, an observation of the structural distortions, range of motion, and the soft tissue palpation. Massage therapy may be covered by some insurance plans if prescribed by a licensed medical doctor or performed in a doctor's office. Further on, I will discuss massage therapy more in-depth since I am very familiar with this field.

Most people are familiar with how a chiropractor approaches the treatment of pain. By manipulating the spine, a chiropractor can alleviate the painful pressure on the spine's nerves by resetting the spinal bones pressing against those nerves. Using heat, cold, traction, and electrical modalities, chiropractors can complement their spinal manipulations. Keep in mind that there are many modalities used in chiropractic, and each chiropractor will use those modalities they feel comfortable with and they feel are effective in treating back pain. Chiropractors, even though considered alternative medicine, can prescribe x-rays and MRIs. Many private and government insurance plans cover them.

Homeopathic practitioners will treat back pain with plant-based formulas to relieve pain and to restore homeostasis. They are often an adjunct to chiropractic, acupuncture, and massage therapy, although both chiropractors and acupuncturists often offer homeopathic formulas in their treatment plan.

I am not that familiar with naturopathic medicine, so I am reluctant to discuss this field in depth. They are rarely state licensed, and I don't believe they come under any health insurance policies. Please feel free to investigate on your own. I know they are very skilled and well trained in massage, homeopathy, acupuncture, manipulation, and nutrition.

Complementary Practices

The primary complementary practices are yoga and Pilates. The first two practices should only be sought out when you are comfortably out of pain and your flexibility/strength is somewhat restored. These two practices will focus on reestablishing flexibility and strength and integrating body movement. Yoga specifically will focus on unimpeded whole-body energy flow. There is a specialized field in yoga called rehabilitative yoga, and perhaps this is best for you coming out of an episode. Be very careful not to take a yoga course that is too advanced for your condition. I recommend Iyengar yoga for people with restricted movement issues. This style of yoga is not easily found but is worth the search. Be sure that Iyengar accredits the Iyengar teacher.

Your goals should be twofold. Number one, find ways to relieve your back pain symptoms, and number two, get to its cause, and then treat the cause. You must treat the cause or causes to prevent pain from returning or, if it does, with less frequency and less down time. You are the important one, the sufferer. You should expect positive results no matter what choices you make. If what you are doing isn't working, stop and switch either the practitioner or the medical field itself. Do not judge an entire field of medicine based on one practitioner's success or not. Ask yourself what isn't working and why. Is it the provider's approach? The incompetence? The modalities used? Or ask if it's "me" who is preventing my complete healing. What emotions or stresses are you holding on to? You must be honest with yourself. Again, I emphasize the importance of understanding your back pain's emotional components to acquire the knowledge and tools to manage these emotions. You can accomplish this through many avenues, such as psychotherapy and spiritual therapies.

Massage Therapy

Being a massage therapist, I will define this medical field in more depth. First, let me proudly state that massage therapists are unique and special healers. Massage therapists heal mainly with their hands and loving energy. Just think about that for a moment. Massage therapists rely on their hands and energy and not on injections, contraptions, pills, or surgery. They can release deep emotional and physical pain from the body's tissues. The wisdom for healing by hands is as ancient as time itself. People needing human touch is innate and natural. Human touch is a necessity for a healthy mind-body and healthy life. This fact is scientifically based. It not only applies to the animal species of humans but all of the animal species on earth. To touch and be touched is as crucial to our health as water and air.

Choosing the correct massage therapy for your back pain must come down to the pain's quality and quantity. In other words, how severe is the pain, how long has it been present, what caused the problem, and how often does the pain come?

All massage therapists are trained to relieve mild, occasional back pain caused by stress or mild trauma, even if they are inexperienced and entry-level therapists. The go-to massage for mild back pain and muscle tightness is the Swedish massage, sometimes called therapeutic massage or spa massage. For back pain that is severely acute or subacute, you need to seek a massage therapist with more specific skills and training. In my personal opinion, there are three main fields of massage geared toward severe, reoccurring back pain. They are neuromuscular bodywork, myofascial structural integrative bodywork, and sports massage. There is a thin gray line separating the three modalities, and often a massage therapist can integrate them simultaneously in the treatment program.

Modern-day massage therapists are more knowledgeable and more advanced than ever before. They can incorporate into their treatment isolated muscle stretching, Kinesio taping, electronic modalities, craniosacral therapy, trigger-point release, and cupping, just to name just a few. Recently two massage practices have been created by massage therapists. They are medical massage and orthopedic massage. These two fields are for those therapists who choose to work closely with a medical doctor. However, their education is still in neuromuscular bodywork and myofascial structural integrative bodywork. Do not be confused with deep tissue massage. Medically, in itself, it means absolutely nothing. Any massage technique that applies deep pressure to the body can be called "deep tissue." It is more of a marketing strategy than a method.

If you are a back sufferer with repeated episodes or have severe back pain, are recently traumatized, or are postsurgical and medically compromised, only see an advanced bodyworker/massage therapist with experience and education. How to determine if a massage therapist is truly advanced, educated, and experienced is your responsibility. Do not use as criteria the cost of the massage or the word of the therapist. It is up to you to research your chosen therapist.

You have the internet to see reviews and web sites. You have word-of-mouth referrals to rely on, and most importantly, you can and should interview a prospective massage therapist by phone before making an appointment. You can do all of this while recuperating at home. The therapist should avail to you all of their continuing education certificate hours, what specific skills they know and use, and how many years they have been in practice.

An advanced massage therapist should have minimally one hundred to five hundred hours of specialized education in one of the above recommended three fields. Experience can also be a factor in choosing the right therapist for your back pain. I believe a massage therapist needs to have three years of basic massage experience and at least one year of specialized practice. Acquiring touch sensitivity and knowledge of the human condition takes time and patience for a massage therapist.

Another factor in choosing a massage therapist is cost. The cost of a massage is not reflective of the efficacy and the skill set of the therapist. Massages now range anywhere from $45 an hour to $180 an hour. It's the wild, wild west when it comes to the massage profession. In choosing a massage therapist, only consider a therapist's skills, education, specialty-certification, experience, and how you relate to them. There isn't a national body of laws and rules in the massage profession. Each state will or will not govern massage therapy as they see fit. There are no rules as to what a massage therapist can charge for their service. One of the best bodywork sessions I ever received was from a very advanced bodyworker who was world-renowned. His charge was $65 for two hours of bodywork.

Authentic certification doesn't guarantee the effectiveness of one advanced therapist over another. Massage therapists are just people and not factory-built robots. If after two or three sessions without satisfying results, let your therapist know how you feel, and maybe that therapist can alter the course of treatment. If you are still not satisfied, move on to another therapist or choose a different massage/bodywork type. More than most, this profession requires a connecting energy exchange between you and your therapist to obtain good results. Massage therapy is unique in that you and your therapist share a very close physical, emotional, and spiritual connection. It is an intimate connection of touch. If you don't feel connected or don't like the therapist, don't return, and look for another therapist.

Suppose you feel that a contributing factor to your back pain is your inability to cope with numerous psychological factors, such as chronic fear, chronic anxiety, and depression, than as an adjunct. In that case, you might consider availing yourself to a licensed mental health counselor or certified metaphysical/spiritual healer.

CHAPTER 9

SELF-CARE

Nutritional Suggestions

- Eat a diet with a wide variety of raw vegetables, fruits, and whole-grain cereals to ensure a complete supply of nutrients for the bones, nerves, and muscles.

- Adequate calcium intake is essential for the repair and rebuilding bones, tendons, cartilage, and connective tissues.

- Fresh pineapples contain bromelain, an enzyme that is excellent in reducing inflammation. If eating fresh pineapples causes a stomach upset, try eating it after meals.

- To relieve cramps and spasms, eat plenty of fruits and vegetables, especially those high in potassium, such as bananas and oranges. Also, drink an adequate amount of warm water and stay hydrated.

- Adequate intake of minerals, such as calcium and potassium, is essential for pain management. Deficiency of these minerals will lead to spasms, cramps, and tense muscles.

- Avoid red meat and seafood in the diet as they contain high uric acid levels, which puts added strain on the kidneys.

- Avoid cold beverages, ice cream, caffeine, sugar, tomatoes, milk, and dairy products.

- Eat mostly cooked or warm foods and beverages. Your stomach is warmth-loving by nature, so eating cold or raw foods (especially nuts and vegetables) and cold drinks can damage stomach functioning over time. Raw fruit is OK as the essence of fruit is very light.

- Not eating dinner later than 6:00 or 7:00 p.m. will give your stomach and other organs a chance to rest and digest! If you eat many heavy foods at night, you are making your stomach work overtime when it should be resting.

- Don't worry. Be happy! Worry, anxiety, and overthinking are the emotions associated with the stomach and spleen, and these emotions in excess have a particular impact on your digestive health.

Stretching, Strengthening, Lifting

- When lifting anything from the ground regardless of its weight, use the legs' powerful hamstring and quadriceps muscles. Bend from the knees and not from the waist. Keep the back straight.

- Stretching and strengthening exercises for the back muscles are essential for long-term back health. Strengthening the abdominal muscles helps reduce strain on the lower back. Strengthening the back muscles will maintain the right tone to those muscles and maintain a good upright posture. For the spine to be in proper alignment, it will need the support of healthy abdominal and back muscles. I recommend seeking a stretching and strengthening professional's guidance rather than going it alone, especially when in a post trauma recovery stage. The resources for this endeavor are endless.

- Gentle movement exercises, such as swimming and walking, are beneficial for back health. I also recommend yoga, tai chi, or Pilates.

Lifestyle Recommendations

- Rub your ears for several minutes a day. This simple massage strengthens kidney function as the ears are connected energetically to the kidney organ and meridian, helping your low back pain.

- A proper balance of work and rest is vital. Eight hours of sleep at night are essential for sound health, and they enable the muscles to recoup from the day's activities.

- While sitting, take a break at least once every hour to alleviate pressure on the vertebrae and disks. Stand up and walk around. Swing from side to side, and let your arms follow the motion. Clasp your hands behind your back, and lift your arms. Do some shoulder rolls. Do the same for the head.

- Weight loss is required to decrease pressure on the joints of the spine, hips, legs, and feet. Carrying lesser weight will help alleviate straining the back muscles trying to hold the upper body up and back.

- Hot baths with Epsom salts help to relax tense muscles and draw toxins from tissues. Rest and relax in the bath for about twenty to thirty minutes, but avoid becoming overtired from the heat and soaking.

- Keep a positive mindset as much as you can, and avoid prolonged periods of anger, hate, blame, and disappointment. Find some quiet time for yourself every day, and reflect on the good in your life. Still the wild beast of stress.

- A smile, even when you are not happy, can change your attitude very quickly. Every day finds something that warms your heart.

Meditation

Pain itself will create tension within the body-mind and has everything to do with what is going on within you; however, outside stress factors can intensify this tension. Start becoming aware of your routine daily living activities, and focus on remaining calm and relaxed and not getting distracted. Focus on living in the present and not in the past or future. Tension starts when you continuously live in the past or future. Impatience and frustration will create stress and tension. Going within and finding a safe, quiet place to focus will help reduce this internal tension.

Meditation is a useful tool to enhance your well-being and help you manage stress by creating a state of calm and tranquility. Find some way and some time each day to meditate, even if it is for five minutes. Long-term results will benefit the mind, body, and emotions. Meditation helps with mental clarity, concentration, enhanced memory, less anxiety, reduced heart rate, reduced blood pressure, and calmer breathing. On an emotional level, meditation will enhance your ability to control and manage negative emotions and result in fewer flare-ups. You will have a stronger sense of inner peace and balance. Being in a peaceful state of mind lets the muscles relax.

There is no need to try to blank out your mind while meditating. Thoughts and distractions are normal while meditating. Simply notice them, but don't engage them. Observe them with a calm and neutral attitude, and let them float away effortlessly. Simply and naturally, bring your focus back to the meditation.

Meditation Helpful Hints

- Meditate before meals and not after.

- Meditate sitting up and not lying down as you will tend to fall asleep.

- Don't meditate in the late evening or before bedtime. The restful alertness from meditation will counteract the dull restlessness of the sleep state.

Counting Breath Meditation

This meditation is easy to learn, requiring no previous experience. Counting breath meditation requires deep breathing and takes only a few minutes to master. This deep breathing is called diaphragmatic breathing. This deep breathing meditation is created by contracting and releasing the diaphragm muscles. There are two diaphragm muscles, each located on either side of the body below the rib cage. These two muscles connect to the abdominal muscles and the lungs, and when contracted, they will open the lung sacs to receive air. When diaphragmic breathing is done correctly, the chest does not expand; only the belly does. Babies naturally push their abdomens in and out while breathing.

When you *inhale,* let your breath come unrestricted and welcomed (receiving mode). When you *exhale,* let your breath leave freely (giving way), taking with it all that is unneeded, unwanted, and unnecessary. Sit in a comfortable position, making sure your body is very supported and that there is no effort needed to make you more comfortable. If required, use props, such as pillow, cushions, and blankets. Close your eyes.

Inhale, taking a long, slow, deep belly breath, and mentally count to four. Hold the breath for a count of two. Exhale the breath for *double* the inhale count or for eight. Before the next inhale, count to two. This is one mini cycle. Inhale and begin the cycle again. Repeat this sequence ten times. You can increase the sequence repetitions as needed. For more significant results, meditate twice a day. The effects are cumulative. Each session will last ten to fifteen minutes.

Sleep Routines

Tips for a Sound Sleep

- Make your sleeping place as comfortable as possible, and go to bed exclusively for sleeping. Keep your office and paperwork out of the bedroom.

- Make sure your mattress is comfortable and supportive. The one you have been using for years may have exceeded its life expectancy—about nine or ten years for most good quality mattresses. The pillow and the mattress need to work together to support the body. The natural spinal curve of the lower back and the neck should be supported when on your back. The lumbar spinal curve should not flatten, and the head should not push forward. The spine should remain straight when sleeping on your side.

- It is essential that the bedroom be attractive and inviting for sleep and free from allergens. Avoid slipping or falling when you get up during the night by removing intrusive objects. The sleeping environment should be cool, dark (free from any light), and quiet. Check your room for noises or other distractions. If your bed partner keeps you awake with loud snoring or air gasps, have them evaluated for sleep apnea. Consider using blackout curtains, eyeshades, earplugs, humidifiers, fans, and ambient sleep machines for a peaceful sleep.

- Separate your sleep time right before bed from activities that can cause excitement, stress, or anxiety. A relaxing routine eliminates bright lights, curling up with a book, listening to calming music, or taking a warm bath. This routine will signal the body that it's time to settle down. Avoid watching TV or looking at your laptop, tablet, or smartphone before bed since those activities will trigger your brain to stay awake.

- Stick to a regular sleep schedule of the same bedtime and wake up time, even on weekends, so your body can adjust to a sleep/wake-up rhythm. Keeping a routine helps to regulate your body's circadian rhythm and helps you to fall asleep and stay asleep for the night.

- Avoid consuming stimulants like coffee, tea, nicotine, or alcohol before bedtime. The latter helps to fall asleep but can disturb the sleep rhythm significantly.

- Avoid cigarettes and heavy meals in the evening. Eating big or spicy meals can cause discomfort from indigestion that can make it hard to sleep. If you can, avoid eating large meals for two to three hours before bedtime. Try a light snack forty-five minutes before bed if you're still hungry.

- After a day of work, you need to wind down to put your body and mind in a sleep mode. The best way is to exercise before bedtime. Walking is an effective relaxing exercise.

- Avoiding bright light in the evening and exposing yourself to sunlight in the morning will keep your circadian (body's natural energy clock) rhythm in sync.

- Pharmacological sleeping pills may make you addicted and lead to other sleep disorders. Natural, gentle alternatives, such as hops or valerian, are preferred.

- If you can't sleep, go into another room and do something relaxing until you feel tired. It is best to take work materials, computers, and televisions out of the sleeping environment. Use your bed only for sleep and sex to strengthen the association between bed and sleep. If you associate a particular activity or item with anxiety about sleeping, omit it from your bedtime routine.

Health is a choice we make every minute of our day. Our self-talk will either sabotage us or enhance our experience on this earth. Be mindful of your body, your mind, and your spirit.

ABOUT THE AUTHOR

Arnie Holtz, is a retired massage therapist with twenty-nine years of experience in massage therapy, almost all in the practice of advanced bodywork. He was a nationally certified CORE Structural Integration Bodyworker. His work focused on creating a body structure more conducive to improved balance, increased function, effortless movement, and better health. He combined myofascial connective tissue structural bodywork, craniosacral, microcurrent, neuromuscular, laser, Kinesio taping, and isolated muscle stretching to reach his clients' goals. He taught hands-on massage and structural bodywork to massage therapists. While his clients came from all walks of life, they all had one thing in common: the need to improve their health.